To Connie and Roscoe Blanchard, and Isobel Shooter

N. D.

To Sam and Chloe

M. F.

Text copyright © 2007 by Nicola Davies
Illustrations copyright © 2007 by Michael Foreman

First U.S. edition 2007

Library of Congress Cataloging-in-Publication Data is available.

Library of Congress Catalog Card Number pending

ISBN 978-0-7636-3364-6

2 4 6 8 10 9 7 5 3 1

Printed in Singapore

This book was typeset in Garamond Ludlow.
The illustrations were done in watercolor and pastel.

Candlewick Press
2067 Massachusetts Avenue
Cambridge, Massachusetts 02140

visit us at www.candlewick.com

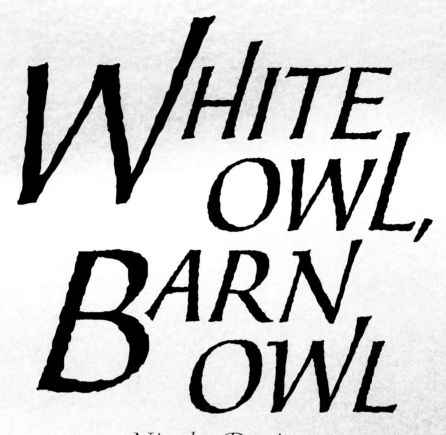

White Owl, Barn Owl

Nicola Davies

illustrated by Michael Foreman

CANDLEWICK PRESS
CAMBRIDGE, MASSACHUSETTS

One frosty winter day,

I helped my grandpa make a big wooden box.

"What's it for, Grandpa?"

"It's for the barn owls to nest in," he said.

"What barn owls?" I asked.

But Grandpa just smiled.

"Wait and see," he said.

We carried the box across the tussocky field.

Barn owls like to nest
in old farm buildings or hollow
tree trunks. Where there aren't any,
they will use a nest box instead.

Grandpa put the box

high in the old oak tree.

"How do you know there are

barn owls here?" I asked.

"I've seen one sitting on that

branch at night," Grandpa said.

"Look! It's left something behind."

Under the branch was a pile of

little sausage-shaped blobs. They

looked like dried poop, but

Grandpa said they were pellets.

Barn owl pellet,
real size

Barn owls have favorite perches that they come back to again and again.

"The owls spit them out," Grandpa said,

"to get rid of the fur and bones they can't eat."

He pulled a pellet apart and showed me

the tiny bones and skulls inside.

Owls swallow their
prey whole; that's why they need to
spit out the bones and fur.

"Will the owl come to our box tonight?"

"Maybe," said Grandpa, "maybe not. Owls are wild

birds. You can't be sure what they'll do."

10

In winter, barn owls have to fly
miles every night to hunt enough
food, so it's hard to find them then.

When the sun went down, we kept a lookout
just in case . . . but we didn't see anything.
"We'll have to be patient," said Grandpa.

We were patient
lots of times!

I thought we'd
never see an owl.

13

And then, one spring night,
just as the sky went pink,
a pale face looked out
of our box. . . .

An owl!

A white owl!

A barn owl!

14

In spring and summer,
owls stay close
to their nests.

And then Grandpa did a strange thing. He put his hand over his mouth and made a loud squeaky sound.

Right away the owl took off and flew toward us. "He thinks I'm a vole or mouse in the grass," Grandpa whispered. "He's coming to see if he can catch his dinner!"

I just held my breath. The owl's whiteness gleamed, and its face was like a pearly heart.

A barn owl's huge eyes can see when it's too dark for human eyes to work. The heart-shaped ruff around the barn owl's face helps to guide sound to its super-sharp ears, which are just holes under the feathers on its head.

Under their feathers, owls are slim. Their bones are hollow, which keeps their bodies light and makes flying easy.

The owl came closer and closer, then landed in the tree — right by our hiding place! It was so light, it hardly bent the twig it perched on.

I could see the tiny ruff of feathers around its face, like stiff lace. I could see the speckled browns on its back. I could see the shine of its big dark eyes. I could have reached out to touch its velvety softness.

And then it raised its wings
like an angel and took off.
It was so quiet, all I heard
was my own heart beating.

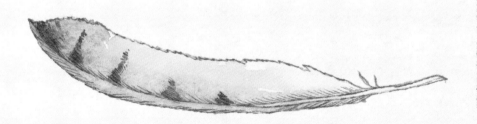

Owls' wing feathers are especially
soft, so owls can move through the air
silently and fly up to their prey
without being heard.

20

Barn owls catch their prey
by pouncing with their long legs
and needle-sharp talons.

The owl flew back and forth over the field. Then another owl came to join it. "That's its mate," Grandpa whispered.

One owl dropped to the ground and came up again. "Look! Look, Grandpa! It's caught something!" I said.

The owl flew straight to the box and went inside.

Hissssss, snorrre, twitter, twitter, hiss. Snoorrrrre.

The weirdest noises came from Grandpa's box.

Barn owls lay up to six eggs, which hatch one after another.
The first chicks to hatch are the biggest, and the
last to hatch are the smallest.

"They've got a family!" Grandpa whispered.

"That's the baby owls squabbling over their dinner."

I held Grandpa's hand, and we
walked home as the moon came up.
"Will the barn owls always nest in
our box now, Grandpa?" I said.
Grandpa smiled. "You know,"
he said, "I think they might."

Barn owls
will come back to
the same nest site year
after year if it stays safe and
there is enough to eat nearby.

27

A NEST BOX NOTE

*O*n modern farms, the open grassland where barn owls like to hunt is often plowed up, and old trees and barns where they can nest are taken down. So barn owls have become rarer. One way to help bring them back is to put up nest boxes.

*T*he barn owl nest box in this book is very sturdy and weather-proof so it will last outside in a tree, but nest boxes inside barns, protected from wind and rain, can be very simple: just an old crate will do! All nest boxes should be 10 to 15 feet up, to be safe from

predators and people, and should have nothing in the way of the entrance, so that the owls can fly right in.

You can get information about how to make a nest box and where to put it from your local wildlife protection organizations. Sometimes it takes a while for owls to use a new nest box, but be patient, and you could have a barn owl family in your box!

INDEX

Look up the pages to find out about all these barn owl things.
Don't forget to look at both kinds of words — this kind and *this kind*.